MAHALIA
Gospel Singer

MAHALIA
Gospel Singer

Kay McDearmon

Illustrated by Nevin and Phyllis Washington

DODD, MEAD & COMPANY, NEW YORK

ACKNOWLEDGMENTS

I am especially grateful for the assistance of Richard B. Allen of the Tulane University Library and Collin B. Hamer, Jr., of the New Orleans Public Library.

Library of Congress Cataloging in Publication Data

McDearmon, Kay.
    Mahalia, gospel singer.

    SUMMARY: A brief biography of the renowned gospel
singer who hoped, through her art, to break down some of
the barriers between black and white people.
    1. Jackson, Mahalia, 1911-1972—Juvenile literature.
[1. Jackson, Mahalia, 1911-1972.   2. Singers]
I. Washington, Nevin.   II. Washington, Phyllis.
III. Title
ML3930.J2M2   783.7   [B]   [92]   75-33882
ISBN 0-396-07280-1

To Rosemary

S HE WAS a tall, beautiful, black woman from the Deep South.

Her grandparents were born into slavery and never left Louisiana. But she traveled all over the world, bringing joy to blacks and whites alike with her glorious singing. Along the way she sang for presidents and kings.

She became a voice of freedom as well. An admirer called her "the single most powerful black woman in the United States."

She was Mahalia Jackson, queen of the gospel singers.

Few famous women began life in such poverty. She was born in 1911 in the slums of New Orleans. Whenever a train roared by, it rattled the windows of the family's three-room shack. There was never a rug on the floor, and the roof leaked. As a small child, Mahalia bathed in a tin tub in the kitchen. And most of the time she ran around barefoot.

8

By day her father loaded cotton onto boats docked in
the nearby Mississippi River. At night and on Saturdays
he did barbering. On Sundays he preached at the Holiness
church close by. Altogether, his pay was too meager to
support his family of six children.

So, to help pay their expenses, Mahalia's pretty mother,
Charity, cleaned house for a wealthy white family. Even

9

so, there wasn't any money left for extras. Mahalia never had a doll, and the children went without toys or a tree even at Christmas.

"Little Haley," though, did get more than her share of love and affection. She was a lively, friendly, and happy child, and she herself said she was the family pet. Three of her aunts lived close by. They visited often, and always hugged Mahalia warmly.

One day when Mahalia was only five years old, her thin, overworked mother became ill. Her doctor tried various medicines, but none of them helped, and she soon died.

Afterward, Mahalia's aunts in New Orleans divided the children among them. Mahalia and her ten-year-old brother Peter went to live with their Aunt Duke and Uncle Emmanuel.

Aunt Duke could seldom afford to buy Mahalia a dress. Another aunt supplied most of her dresses. They were castoffs from a rich white family she worked for as a servant.

On Saturdays Mahalia went to the barber shop to visit her father. He bounced her on his knee and gave her whatever money he could spare for her needs. Sometimes

it was as little as fifteen cents because he had married again and needed his earnings for the new family he was raising.

On weekday mornings, before going to her own school for blacks, Mahalia helped dress the children of a white family for school.

Mahalia often rose at sunrise. After breakfast she

helped her uncle weed the garden. There they raised their own vegetables—beans, okra, corn, tomatoes, peas, mustard greens, cabbage, and pumpkins. Another of Mahalia's chores was feeding the chickens, pigeons, and goats.

Aunt Duke worked outside her home as a cook. She was a wonderful cook, and she taught Mahalia how to

bake corn bread and biscuits. She also learned to cook tasty turtle soup and chitlins. Chitlins are the small intestines of pigs. To Mahalia they were "the sweetest part of the hog."

On special days Aunt Duke would allow her to make pralines—a favorite candy in the South—mostly from sugar and pecans.

For their dinner Mahalia and her uncle often caught shrimps and crabs by the bucketful in the Mississippi River.

The swamps were close by, too, and sometimes Mahalia, Peter, and her uncle hunted alligators there. When they spied a small alligator one of them would give it a sharp blow on the head with a pole. The next day Aunt Duke would serve baked alligator tail seasoned with garlic and herbs for their breakfast.

When they needed firewood for the kitchen stove, Mahalia helped to collect it. Sometimes Peter helped, too, but he was usually away doing yard work for a white family.

With an axe Mahalia cut wood from old abandoned barges that had begun to sink into the mud near the river. Armed with a long pole, she also fished logs out of the

water. After chopping them, she dropped them into her wheelbarrow.

Some days she wandered along the railroad tracks, picked up chunks of coal that had spilled from the partly open coal cars, and dumped them into her basket. This way she helped to fill the family coal bin for the winter.

Mahalia played with her sisters, brothers, cousins, and the other poor children in her neighborhood. Among them were some white youngsters. They all romped together without thought of any difference in color.

Sometimes they walked to Audubon Park and rode the merry-go-round. They hitched rides now and then on a train's caboose and rode to the sugar factory. There for only a few pennies they could get the juicy sugar cane stalks they loved to chew.

Often Mahalia and her playmates just sat on the grassy river levee and watched the steamboats go by. As they watched, they sang "I'm Forever Blowing Bubbles" or "When the Saints Come Marching In."

More than anything, Mahalia loved to sing. From the

time she began going to her neighborhood black Baptist church, she sang hymns with the members, clapping her hands and tapping her feet along with them. She had been only about five years old when the minister asked her to join the choir. "I had a big voice even then," Mahalia remembered later.

Two of her father's relatives, who did a comedy act with Ma Rainey's Rabbit Foot Minstrels, heard little Mahalia sing one day. They were really impressed with her voice. They begged Aunt Duke to let her travel and sing with their black minstrel show in one-night stands in big tents all around the South.

"I can't let her do that," her aunt said firmly. "Mahalia's much too young to travel."

Aunt Duke also feared if the child joined the act, she might even forget to attend church. This would distress her aunt, because her greatest hope was to raise Mahalia to be a strong Baptist like herself. As it was, she was happy that the youngster was already using her fine voice to praise the Lord.

Besides, Aunt Duke was against any kind of show business. To her, the blues were sinful, and she knew that Ma Rainey was a blues singer.

18

Those days New Orleans was bursting with music. Mahalia heard dock workers singing as they loaded cargo onto riverboats. She heard the lively hymn singing at the Holiness church nearby. She heard brass bands playing on street corners to advertise fish fries. And from open windows she heard phonograph records wail out the blues.

Bessie Smith, the most famous blues singer of them

all, was Mahalia's idol. She especially liked to hear her sing the "St. Louis Blues."

As Bessie began, "I hate to see that evening sun go down," Mahalia listened carefully. She also dreamed a little, whispering to herself, "Someday the sun will shine down on me in some faraway place."

As a teen-ager, Chicago was her idea of a faraway place. Her Uncle Emmanuel had worked there as a bricklayer, and told her about the better life there. Ever since, she was anxious to go and see for herself. Why, in Chicago blacks could even shop in the same stores as whites!

Meanwhile, in school Mahalia had learned to read, write, and do arithmetic well. Some days she had walked miles after school to scrub floors for a dime. But she hadn't been able to save much money.

Still, when she was in the eighth grade she asked Aunt Duke to allow her to go to Chicago. When she refused, Mahalia decided to quit school. She had gone as far as most of the black children did in New Orleans at that time.

Now she could spend all her time earning enough money to go to Chicago. Some days she worked ten hours baby-sitting or washing and ironing clothes in

white folks' homes. Before long she could iron a man's shirt in three minutes, and she was proud of that skill.

One day when Mahalia was sixteen, her Aunt Hannah came to visit. She hoped to take her tall, strong, beautiful niece back to Chicago to live with her.

Now more than ever, Mahalia wanted to go there. She had just seen an advertisement in a newspaper offering nurses' training to black girls in a Chicago hospital. She wanted to become a nurse, and she couldn't get the training in New Orleans. And she feared if she stayed, she would likely always be just somebody's servant.

Aunt Duke was afraid that in Chicago Mahalia would drift away from the teachings of her Baptist religion. So she still opposed her going. Much as Mahalia hated to displease her aunt, she decided to go anyway. When Aunt Duke saw how strong her feelings were, she reached for the box where she kept Mahalia's savings and gave them to her.

On the train trip north, Mahalia and Aunt Hannah nibbled on home-cooked fried chicken, yams, and biscuits that they had brought along in a basket.

Once they arrived in Chicago, Mahalia was surprised that a white taxi driver would accept them as passengers. It could never happen in New Orleans at that time.

As her Aunt Hannah asked, he drove them to the South Side, a section where her neighbors for miles around were mostly black.

Here in Chicago the pay for black workers was higher than in New Orleans. Some of the blacks living there drove their own cars; some were buying their own homes;

and a few even owned restaurants, drugstores, barber shops, and apartment buildings.

Aunt Hannah lived in a large, rented apartment. She shared it with her sister—Mahalia's Aunt Alice—her little boy and girl, and a renter. Mahalia slept on a sofa on the sun porch. And to help pay for their rent and food both her aunts worked as cooks.

Mahalia had been in Chicago only a short time when her Aunt Hannah had a heart attack. The doctor said she would need to rest at home for at least several weeks. So, instead of starting to train to become a nurse, Mahalia had to go to work to help with the expenses.

She found a job doing laundry for a white family. On wintry mornings she rose at six o'clock and rode the elevated train to the North Side, shivering in her sweater. As soon as she could she bought a fleece-lined coat to shield herself from the blizzardy weather.

Much of her spare time Mahalia spent in activities at the Greater Salem Baptist Church. She decided to join the choir, and for her tryout she sang "Hand Me Down a Silver Trumpet, Gabriel." She was happy that "everybody liked the way I sang it." Before long, she was singing solos for the choir.

24

When the minister's sons formed the Johnson Gospel Singers, she joined them. The group quickly became popular singing at black churches in the area. Soon Mahalia's warm, rich voice brought her invitations from these churches to sing alone.

As a teen-ager, she never hoped to make singing her career. But she saved money to take lessons from a black concert singer. Professor DuBois began by asking her to sing "Standing in the Need of Prayer." She had hardly started singing the spiritual when he stopped her. "You are singing too loud," he said. "Try singing softly."

Mahalia much preferred "making a joyful noise unto the Lord." So she never returned for another lesson.

The larger black churches in Chicago also found fault with Mahalia's style at first. Sometimes as she belted out her gospel songs with a rocking beat, clapping her hands and moving her body, her combs flew out of her hair. When the spirit moved her she dropped to her knees, or even ran and skipped down the church aisles.

Mahalia soon won over the larger churches. She nailed up signs on fences and telephone poles, charged a dime to cover her expenses, and sang her gospel songs in basement churches. When her bouncy singing drew overflow crowds, the other churches gladly welcomed her.

Before long, Mahalia was invited to sing in black churches as far away as St. Louis, a distance of about three hundred miles. She caught the night train, sat up all night, and returned to work in Chicago the next day.

One night Mahalia was sitting with a friend, counting her share of the evening's money, when she suddenly

realized that she could buy a doll. "I always wanted a doll when I was a child," she said, "but we were too poor to buy any toys." Mahalia was delighted when at a dinner honoring her later, a little nine-year-old Chicago girl gave her a doll.

A business depression swept the United States in the early 1930s, and the buying power of rich and poor alike dropped sharply. The stock market crashed. Banks failed. Millions of people lost their jobs. In large cities blacks were often among the first to lose theirs.

Mahalia fared better than most. She kept getting calls to sing at more black churches. Sometimes she'd be away from Chicago for a week at a time "singing for her supper" and for her share of the nickels and dimes dropped into the collection boxes. When she returned home she usually could get work as a hotel maid.

On her way home from work one day she saw a line of hungry people, waiting for free bread. She asked them to come with her, stopped at a grocery store, and with her day's pay bought smoked ribs and potatoes. Then she took the strangers home and cooked supper for them all.

In the midst of the depression, when she was twenty-five, Mahalia married Isaac Hockenhull. He was a well-educated man, but in those hard times he couldn't find a job where he could use what he learned about chemistry in college. Sometimes the post office called him to help them on days when they needed extra mail carriers.

Proud as Isaac was of Mahalia's talents, he complained that she was wasting them singing gospel songs. So one day when a Chicago newspaper announced a contest for parts in *The Jazz Mikado*, an all-black musical play, he urged her to enter. Because both of them were out of work at the time, she agreed to try.

With her singing of "Sometimes I Feel Like a Motherless Child," Mahalia easily won a leading role. But when she came home, her husband had found a job, so she gave up the part.

Mahalia kept singing for the Lord. But, as her gospel singing began to take her to churches and tents all across the country, Isaac was unhappy about coming home to an empty apartment.

Meanwhile, Mahalia found that Isaac liked to gamble. As a deeply religious person, this caused her much distress. Sadly, they agreed, after seven years of marriage, to separate.

Those days she was glad she was so busy. It helped her to forget about her broken marriage.

Besides singing for live audiences, Mahalia had begun making records of her religious songs. Her first Decca record, "God's Gonna Separate the Wheat from the Tares," was a hit among blacks in the South.

Then in 1946 for Apollo she recorded "Moving on Up a Little Higher," a spiritual she had loved since she was a child. Blacks from coast to coast bought this record. Altogether, over two millon copies were sold. Mahalia was now queen of the gospel singers.

Famous black entertainers tempted her with offers to sing with their bands. But she turned them all down, even Louis Armstrong. "I have no desire to sing the blues," she said. "They are too sad. I prefer to sing songs of hope and faith."

In 1950, Mahalia was thrilled when she was invited to give her first concert at Carnegie Hall in New York. But she was afraid, too. She knew that all the great musical artists appeared there. Suppose when she stood up in that famous hall she couldn't sing a note!

But when she saw her audience, still mostly blacks, she wasn't frightened any more. They broke the hall's

30

attendance records, spilling over onto the stage, hardly leaving room for Mahalia. When she sang, some people wept. A few even fainted.

After this triumph, Mahalia's career kept "moving on up," and what she called her "singing weight" climbed to two hundred pounds. She toured the country's concert halls, winning the hearts of new millions, now both black and white. And in her long, flowing robes she gave as many as two hundred concerts a year.

She also sang for the Empress of Japan, and for several presidents. Once she sang in the White House for President Eisenhower on his birthday, and at a party for John F. Kennedy the night before he became president.

Backstage before each program Mahalia read from her Bible, and her strong faith shone through when she sang. As she poured out her soul in "I Believe," it was clear to her huge audiences that she did believe the words she sang.

Whenever she was in Chicago, she even took the time to read the Bible to the neighborhood children.

Mahalia's religious records spread her fame abroad, and "I Can Put My Trust in Jesus" won a prize from the French Academy of Music. Wherever she sang during her tour of Europe in 1952 she was accepted as a great artist.

Danish children gave her so many flowers that they filled her hotel lobby. In Norway twenty thousand fans bought her recording of "Silent Night." And she gave a command performance for the king and queen of Sweden.

"People everywhere loved my gospel music," Mahalia

said, "even though they didn't understand a word of English."

Mahalia was happy that white audiences everywhere accepted her as a singer. When she returned to the United States she hoped that white people would now also accept her as a person, and treat her as they treated each other. But in this hope she was to be disappointed.

When she toured the South in her car, many restaurants still refused to serve her. Some gas stations wouldn't sell her any gas, and wouldn't even allow her to use their rest rooms. To get a place to sleep Mahalia had to drive into black neighborhoods.

Still, there were times when people were kind. Once, when a waitress in Alabama blocked Mahalia's way into a restaurant, a white truck driver rushed out to her car with a bag of sandwiches and coffee.

"I saw what happened," he said, handing her the food. "I hope tomorrow will be better."

Mahalia never thought that anyone would object to seeing or hearing her anywhere on television, as she was an instant success on a local Chicago channel. So one day she suggested that her program be carried over the network, so the whole country could enjoy her songs.

"It's impossible *now*," the manager told her. "Our

sponsors would be afraid to have a black on a program shown in the South."

Racial feeling also marred the memory of one of Mahalia's happiest days. One Christmas she was asked to sing on "Wide, Wide World," a television news and entertainment program. Her songs would be heard all around the nation from the church she attended as a child.

Mahalia rounded up many of her childhood playmates for the event. Together, on Christmas, they sang "Born in Bethlehem" and "Sweet Little Jesus Boy." After the program white people from California to New York telephoned to praise her.

But the next day when she was shopping in downtown New Orleans, she couldn't find a restaurant that would serve her a cold drink.

In some ways Mahalia fared better in the North. Once, to celebrate her appearance on a Chicago television program, the Edgewater Beach Hotel gave a dinner in her honor. Twenty years before she had worked there as a maid!

But when Mahalia wanted to buy a house in a Chicago suburb, she found that though whites enjoyed her singing, they strongly objected to having her as a neighbor.

Threatening telephone calls came day and night. "If you buy that house," one angry white man yelled over the telephone, "I'll bomb it."

Mahalia bought the house, and bullets were fired through a window. To prevent further violence a police guard was stationed around the house for a full year.

This incident alone could have made Mahalia bitter. But she couldn't really hate anyone.

Later, when CBS was planning a television special at her house, she invited all the children in the area.

"Their mothers dressed them up, white and black, and they all came," said Mahalia. "We had a wonderful time. I cooked a Louisiana Everything-Gumbo, red beans, and rice. We all ate—cameramen, children, neighbors, everybody."

Mahalia's warm feelings reached out to all races. She often praised her friend, the Reverend Martin Luther King, Jr., for never preaching hate or violence.

When he became active in trying to secure equal rights for blacks, Mahalia helped in every way she could.

She sang at his rally in a Montgomery, Alabama, church in 1956 to help the blacks win their fight against the bus companies. It was a long and bitter struggle. A year later when it ended, blacks no longer had to sit in the back of the bus in the South.

Mahalia also gave much of her fortune to the civil rights movement. She also sang in special concerts to raise more money. And she began singing "freedom songs" at all her concerts.

Once, at Constitution Hall in Washington, D.C., Mahalia added "America" to her program. Afterward, a black teen-ager came to her dressing room, tears in her eyes.

"How can you sing, 'My country' when you know white people don't want us here?" she asked.

"It *is* our country, too," Mahalia told her. "And if the Lord has taken me off my knees scrubbing floors for others and brought me this far . . . there is hope for all of us. Go back to school, and trust in people like the Reverend Martin Luther King, Jr., to correct things."

Mahalia herself helped to correct things by giving money to help needy, talented young people. In the true Christian spirit she aided whites as well as blacks, assuring them the education she never had.

The highlight of Mahalia's public efforts for her race was her singing at the inspiring March on Washington arranged by black leaders to focus attention on goals yet to be met.

That summer day in 1963 a throng of 200,000 people —black and white—descended upon the capital of the United States by plane, train, bus, and automobile. One man roller-skated from Chicago. Another man bicycled all the way from Ohio.

Around noon, young and old started parading to the Lincoln Memorial. As they marched they sang hymns. They also waved flags, banners, and signs in support of equal freedom for all Americans.

Mahalia stood on the marble steps near the statue of Abraham Lincoln and gazed out upon the well-mannered crowd. In her deep, powerful voice she started singing "I've been 'buked and I've been scorned." As she raised the tempo of the old spiritual, and began clapping her hands, the vast crowd sang and clapped with her.

Martin Luther King followed her soul-stirring singing with his great "I Have a Dream" speech. In it he foresaw the day when people of all races would be treated equally in this country.

Mahalia fulfilled one of her own dreams when she toured the Holy Land, and saw the birthplace of Christ. In Jerusalem, Christians, Jews, and Arabs alike were moved by the magic of her gospel singing.

Over the years Mahalia conquered the concert world, but she didn't forget blacks who hadn't fared as well as she. Once she gave all the ticket money from a Chicago concert to local gospel singers. Another time she sang to enable South Side children to go to summer camp.

Whenever she could she slipped away into big city

ghettos and lifted the spirits of many poor blacks there with her fiery gospel singing. And she cheered people in hospitals and prisons.

One wintry night after she sang in a South Side church, a woman rushed up to Mahalia. "My poor mother is very sick," she said. "Would you come over to my house and sing just one song for her?"

Mahalia didn't hesitate. In the bitter cold she walked

along with the stranger, and climbed up a long stairway to her apartment. There Mahalia gladdened the mother's heart by singing several of her favorite gospel songs just for her.

In her later years the strain of so much singing and traveling began to tell. At times Mahalia had to rest her weary body in hospitals, and doctors warned her against taking long trips out of the country. Yet, in 1971, she flew overseas to entertain American soldiers. When she was in Germany she collapsed on the stage.

Her tired heart stopped beating on January 27, 1972. As one of her millions of admirers said at her funeral, "Mahalia made life more beautiful and joyous for us all."

The Author

KAY MCDEARMON was born in San Francisco and received her B.A. degree from the University of California at Berkeley. Before devoting her time to writing, she was a high school teacher and social service worker.

Mrs. McDearmon lives with her husband, a professor of Speech Pathology, in Turlock, California, where leisure time activities include bicycling, swimming, reading, and music.

She is the author of *A Day in the Life of a Sea Otter* and *The Walrus: Giant of the Arctic Ice*.

The Illustrators

NEVIN AND PHYLLIS WASHINGTON met while students at the School of Visual Arts in Manhattan and married shortly after their graduation.

Mahalia, Gospel Singer marks the first children's book they have illustrated. During the short time since they began their career in commercial art, their work has appeared in a number of magazines including *Analog Science Fact and Science Fiction Magazine*. The Washingtons live and work in New York City.